# Agile Explained

# Agile Explained

## An Overview of the Values and Benefits of Agile

AL KRAUS

ISBN-13: 9781548020064
ISBN-10: 1548020060
Library of Congress Control Number: 2017909357
CreateSpace Independent Publishing Platform
North Charleston, South Carolina

*This book is dedicated to Karen and Julie. You both are the reasons I continually try to become a better man.*

*Thank you.*

# Contents

# Preface

You may be wondering why I am writing this book or even whom I am writing this book for. I admit, I enjoy working with an inquisitive audience, and these two excellent questions are linked to some degree. Let's see if I can answer them to your satisfaction.

I am writing this book because I truly believe in the power of the Agile process. In the software-development field, we've learned many valuable lessons by applying the values and practices of Agile. The good news is that any department or business field can also apply those same lessons and use the same helpful tools to make work easier, allowing for greater productivity.

Of course, many books have already been written about Agile software development and the frameworks I mention in this book. These books are written by talented authors, and I am not trying to replace them. However, I have concluded that these books are typically written for people within software development. As such, the writers have made certain assumptions concerning the reader's basic knowledge of Agile.

This leads into the answer for the second question: there appears to be a shortage of introductory books for people outside of software development. These people may have heard of Agile or even some of its benefits. However, some of the technical terms and explanations concerning engineering practices mean little, if anything, to them. This is the audience I hope to reach with *Agile Explained*. An audience from outside of software development who would like to understand the basics of not only what Agile is but also how they could start to use it themselves. All this, of course, without being drowned in a sea of rhetoric and technical jargon.

If you happen to be in this target audience, this book is for you! If you are not, then why not continue reading anyway? You might find something useful.

So, sit back and allow me to take you through the wonderful world of Agile. I will attempt to keep things concise, helpful, and hopefully even a little entertaining.

# Introduction

Agile software development has been around since the mid-1990s. Pioneers in this emerging field gathered in 2001 and created the *Agile Manifesto* to compile the lessons they learned while experimenting with better ways of creating software. These visionaries brought together different ideas on how to increase productivity and efficiency. The ideas became the basis of the Agile philosophy using the manifesto as its foundation. The *Agile Manifesto* has four values and twelve principles. The values are included here:

*We are uncovering better ways of developing software by doing it and*
*helping others do it. Through this work we have come to value:*
*Individuals and interactions over processes and tools*
*Working software over comprehensive documentation*
*Customer collaboration over contract negotiation*
*Responding to change over following a plan*
*That is, while there is value in the items on the right, we value*
*the items on the left more.*[i]

From these simple values, many different Agile methodologies and frameworks have been developed. These frameworks specify processes and practices used to encourage and support Agile values. A commonality of these different approaches is that they enable companies from across the world to deliver valuable, higher-quality software faster than with any method from before the Agile movement.

Recently, it has become increasingly evident that the lessons learned in software development can be applied in other aspects of business. So, what is the main hurdle of expanding the principles? Many departments or organizations outside of information technology believe Agile is just for software production. Most books that describe Agile practices use software-development examples, which compound the problem. The result is that, by using the rhetoric of software production to teach Agile, only people from software production have the foundational knowledge to learn how to apply Agile from existing methods.

We in the Agile software-development community have learned our lessons, and it's time for us to become teachers and help others learn from our successes and mistakes. In this book, I attempt to discard the vocabulary commonly used to discuss Agile, to help make it easier to understand. This will also show *how* and *why* these lessons can apply to departments outside the realm of software development. Beginning with basic concepts at the foundation of what it means to be Agile, we will expand into greater detail as we look behind the curtain to understand how these concepts are combined. Finally, we will conclude with suggestions on how you can begin your own Agile journey.

I hope you will join me on this grand adventure into the world of Agile. Come see the values and practices software development has learned over the past couple of decades. And see how these lessons can help your department or possibly even your entire company develop into a learning organization that is constantly improving.

# Part I: Foundations

*Process transforms any journey into a series of small steps, taken one by one, to reach any goal. Process transcends time, teaches patience, rests on a solid foundation of careful preparation, and embodies trust in our unfolding potential.*

—DAN MILLMAN

*You can't build a great building on a weak foundation. You must have a solid foundation if you're going to have a strong superstructure.*

—GORDON B. HINCKLEY

# The Scientific Method

In my experience, if I were to ask you if you have ever heard of the scientific method, your most likely reply would be that you remember it from school. You might not remember the details, but you remember something about it being a process used by countless scientists for centuries that has led to nearly every scientific breakthrough. If you remember more than this, you have an awesome recall from school. If you do not remember, no need to worry, we will cover the main parts you need to know for the purposes of this book.

The scientific method is a simple and effective process. It can be used to explain why something is the way it is and help us discover better ways of doing, well, pretty much anything. For our purposes, though, we will focus on the latter use of the method. Follow me as I walk through with an Agile perspective.

We begin by observing the current state of a process and ask this question: Can this be improved? If so, we formulate a hypothesis for changes we can make to improve the process or environment. We then develop tests we can use to track the impact of the experiment. Once these tests are implemented, we measure to confirm if the change we are testing is improving our original situation. After we implement the change and monitor the effects, we evaluate the results and decide if things are better now with the change. If the change has improved, we keep it. Otherwise, we throw it out. We will begin this cycle of experimentation and observation until we find an idea that improves our original state. By repeating this exercise, we learn that each successful experiment gives us a process that is slightly better than what we started with. When an experiment fails, we learn a great deal as well. In fact, sometimes learning what won't work is just as valuable (if not more) as finding out what will work and could possibly lead us to the next possible improvement.

This same process can be applied to business practices in much the same way. Although a simple idea, it is one of significant impact. This implies that we can take any current business process and continually improve it through experimentation. This kind of improvement can be expanded to other applicable processes, giving your company a significant competitive advantage. This brings us back to an important fundamental point: at its root, Agile is the scientific method applied to business practices. Accepting the premise of continual experimentation and modification sets a strong foundation for the rest of our journey through Agile principles.

Plain and simple—there is always room for improvement. No process or business or project is perfect. Humbling, isn't it? Without the courage to embrace experimentation, even if some experimentation may fail, we cannot hope to find those innovative breakthroughs that will allow us to move to a higher level of productivity. You must be comfortable experimenting with change and accepting the fact that no matter how much we think we know, there is *always* room for improvement. The Agile approach is a proven system to help us find improvements and implement them in our organizations.

# The Four Tenets of Agile

To be considered Agile, a team must have four basic tenets in place. These tenets are embedded in each Agile framework but can also be used on their own. The fundamental practices included in these tenets will help any team begin to see the results that Agile values can bring. These basic practices build on each other, allowing the teams to find innovative ways to improve their own processes. They are as follows:

- Make the work visible.
- Inspect and adapt.
- Limit work in progress.
- Work in small batches.

It is the values expressed in the Agile Manifesto, summarized in these tenets, that should be the main focus. When we get into describing some of the different methodologies later, we will talk about how they implement these basics. A firm understanding of the basics will allow you to customize the practices in those methodologies to best fit your company and team. Without a strong foundation, a team could find that they are doing the practices without any real benefits.

Each improvement is a step that can be used to drive to the next improvement, thus becoming a catalyst for increased effectiveness.

All of the available frameworks for Agile will implement these tenets in different ways and will be covered in detail later. This approach is like progression used in martial arts. In both martial arts I have studied, students learn the basic moves on their first day. From that day forward, in every practice session, the student will continually strive toward perfecting these basic moves. As the student progresses in belt level, he or she gets better at not only the physical moves of the art but also the mental conditioning. This same approach toward incremental change can be applied to learning Agile through these four tenets. Each step along the path can reinforce the direction the team is going and encourage that next step.

Once these tenets are consistently practiced, there are additional things that can be done to increase effectiveness. We will discuss some of these more in-depth topics later in part II, for now, let's concentrate on the foundation. These basic beliefs can be applied to any process that can be observed and measured. Even if it is measured anecdotally. As you read further, some of the ideas presented may seem familiar. I intend to help show you how these ideas can be used to take your teams to the next level. Let's now step through these tenets in more detail.

## Making the Work Visible

Have you ever seen a television show where a team will try to remodel a foreclosed house? Sometimes, the team will luck out, and the home will only need minor improvements. Other times, it's a complete money and time pit, and the team is almost lucky if they can break even. Wouldn't it have been nice if the team had the chance to go inside the foreclosed house and see what they were up against from the beginning? Without some sort of visualization, it is extremely difficult to discern potential areas of improvement. Think back to the scientific method: we need a way to observe and measure. The visual could be as simple as a shared to-do list with a column for everyone on the team. In Agile, a more common approach is the use of a simple columned board, sometimes called a Kanban board. *Kanban* is a Japanese word meaning *billboard* or *sign*. So, a Kanban board is just a sign board. This board can use multiple layouts. We will use a very simple form as our starting point.

The simple Kanban board has three columns. These columns are labeled *Not Started*, *In Progress*, and *Done*. Using this board, we can put an index card for each piece of work that needs to be done in the *Not Started* column. As people on the team begin to work on any item, they add their names to the card and move it to the *In Progress* column. When they are done, they move it to the *Done* column.

This is a very simple approach to visualizing work. You might be asking yourself, "If this is so simple to do, why would people resist doing it?" There are a couple of common reasons that people push back on making their work visible. One of the most common is that team members are so focused on trying to get work done, they assume they do not have the time to make the work visible. When they make this assumption, the result is an abundance of e-mails or status-report meetings so everyone knows what the work is and its associated progress.

Another possible reason for resistance to this visualization is a fear of transparency. In certain corporate cultures, it can be a challenge to feel safe enough to allow transparency into everything you do. Some old-school management styles (e.g., Fredrick Taylor) will try to control their people using fear as a tactic. This can sometimes appear to be an effective tool in the short term. However, the lack of transparency and the overall fear of team members to try new things may prevent the team from maturing and making any serious improvements. These types of corporate cultures also encourage people to hoard information to protect themselves—possibly from losing their positions. The more information they alone have, the more secure they feel. Although this line of thinking can benefit the individual, it has a long-term negative effect on the team and the company. By encouraging team members to share information, the team improves, productivity increases, and team recognition becomes a positive factor. Being recognized as part of a team can replace those individual silos as the whole team now receives accolades for their accomplishments and improvement.

It is important to note that the reasons to resist the visualization of the work are cultural. In fact, the biggest obstacles in trying to increase Agility will be cultural. Therefore, buy-in from management is critical. If managers do not support the cultural changes needed, no transformation will ever be successful. Like so many things worth doing, these tenets are simple but not easy. Management will need to help the team members feel safe enough to share information and embrace transparency. To increase the chances of success in your Agile journey, you should start small and allow increased success to propel you.

Once we start visualizing work, we will be able to make observations on its progress or lack of it. This can help identify bottlenecks in the work flow and point out areas that can be made more efficient as well as steps that are working well. It is also very common at this point to see that team members have multiple items in progress all at the same time. The important thing at this stage is to just make the work visible. This is the foundation we will use going forward to not only help identify areas of improvement but also tell if our experiments are working. It is vital to have this in place so the other tenets can be utilized.

To help illustrate the use of the basic tenets, we will view and discuss a few boards and see what observations we can make. For our fictional examples, we will use a small team. Mike, Sally, and Jason are team members who all report to Sue. The actual text of the work being done is not important for this example, so let's jump right in.

| Ready | In Progress | | Done | |
|---|---|---|---|---|
| | Jason | Jason | Jason | Mike |
| | Sally | Jason | Mike | Mike |
| | Sally | Sally | Sally | |
| | Mike | | | |

Right off the bat, you can see that Sally and Jason both have several items in progress at one time, while Mike only has one. But Mike has more items in the *Done* column than the others. Can you think of any rationale to explain this? One reason could be that Mike just finished several items of work. It could also be that Mike read ahead and already knows the importance of limiting his work in progress. While a quick glance will not give you all the answers, watching the board over time gives you a much better idea of how the work is flowing...or not.

What else can we learn from this figure? We can tell that the team appears to work in isolation. Each member works on his or her own items with little, if any, collaboration. Let me take a moment to explain a subtle difference. A functional work group is any collection of individuals who are put together to accomplish work. They work separately, according to their specialization, to accomplish the work assigned to the group. A team will break out of their specialized roles when needed, pitching in to help get the work done. At this point, one could say Sue's team is more of a functional working group than a team. This may or may not be an issue depending on the type of work being done, but it is something one can observe from the board.

Hopefully this example has started to help you see the benefits of visualization. Let's leave our team for now. We will come back to them in a bit as we discuss our next tenet, where we will help them interpret their board and experiment to find improvements.

## Inspect and Adapt

The actions of inspecting and adapting are the main workhorses of improvement for any team working within the Agile philosophy. All the monitoring in the world will not make teams more effective unless it's acted on. Allowing the team to take the time to periodically inspect how things are going and think about potential improvements is the next step. These introspective moments need to identify anything that is slowing them down or come up with new ideas that could speed things up. Once a potential change has been identified, they need to decide on an experiment that could make an improvement. The team will need to define what both success and failure will look like before they start the experiment. We want to be able to identify the failure as fast as possible to minimize the effect of the failure, and give us the opportunity to try something else. It is extremely important for management to create a culture that is safe for the teams to try new things and, yes, even to fail at these experiments. Without the feeling of safety, teams will be unwilling to attempt some of the ideas they have for improving. Failing an experiment should be a learning opportunity instead of a sign that the team failed. If failed experiments are held against the team, it will stifle creativity and innovation and reduce the team's effectiveness. This safety to try is important because we never know the full effects of an experiment until we put it into practice and observe the results. This is why it is so important to visualize the work and monitor the process. I once had a team where we decided to try a different way of tracking the team's progress in order to have more fun. We used a visualization of a chariot race. The team's progress moved the chariot whenever an item was completed, while a shadow chariot moved at a predetermined constant pace. When we first decided to try it, I thought this was an awesome idea. It turns out, the team got completely confused, and within a week, we threw out the idea. What we learned from it was celebrating successes and experimentation was more fun than what we thought the experiment would give us.

As the team looks back on their recent performance, they should brainstorm different ideas that could potentially improve their processes and then pick one to try. It is then important for the team to decide how the change will be tracked as well as to determine both success and failure criteria for the experiment. It is vital that the failure condition is defined so the team can recognize it as quickly as possible, cancel the experiment, and learn from it. Every failed attempt in this manner allows the team to learn more about what they do and what works for them. Through the monitoring of the process, the team can determine how the change is affecting their productivity. It is not uncommon that some time may need to pass before the team can determine the outcome of the experiment. If the change improves the team's productivity, they accept the change as the new baseline and repeat the process.

Not every experiment attempted by the team needs to improve productivity. Some ideas might be specifically designed to improve morale or other intangibles. One team I worked with decided they wanted to encourage everyone to be on time to meetings. Their experiment was that whenever someone was late, he or she had to put a quarter into a jar. When the jar had enough money, they would order pizza for the team. At first, people complained when they had to pay into the jar, but after the first pizza was bought for the team, deposits into the jar started to slow down. In the meantime, their meetings were starting on time, and morale and engagement increased. If changes like these do not decrease productivity, they can be kept as successful experiments. The increased morale will have a long-term effect of improving engagement and productivity as well as increasing retention.

There are several methods the team can use during these inspection points to come up with ideas for improvement. I will refer to these introspection events as retrospectives. These retrospective meetings are much more effective when they are led by a trained facilitator. Without a facilitator, it is common for the team to use this meeting as a venting session, complaining about things outside the control of the team. The facilitator will help focus the discussions toward constructive topics within the team's control to implement. There are many retrospective games online to keep these sessions fresh. Using different approaches will help prevent the team from getting in a rut.

As long as the team continues to inspect and adapt, improvements will continue and productivity will increase. Allowing for the possibility of short-term pain from failed experiments, long-term gain can be achieved. Encouraging teams to carry on these experiments increases their feeling that management is listening and valuing their opinions brought into the process, and that increases their morale. Supporting this type of behavior can also increase team empowerment—more on that later.

Let's go back to visit Sue and her team again. Sue decides to hold a periodic retrospective once a month. At the first one, the team has a conversation about working on so many things at one time. The reason appears to be that they finish something and move on to the next, but then the first item comes back for a quality issue. The team decides to attempt an experiment, that for the more complicated items, they will have two people work on it, to try to cut down on the quality issues and the rework. They decide that a success would be a decrease in the number of quality issues, and a failure would be if the amount of work produced dipped too low. Let's see how they do with it.

| Ready | In Progress | Done |
|---|---|---|
| | Sally Mike / Jason | Jason Sally / Mike Sally |
| | | Jason / Mike |
| | | Sally / Sally Mike |
| | | Jason Sally / Jason |
| | | Sally |

Well, it appears our team is acting more like a team now. We see that Sally has her name on several cards with Mike and Jason. There also appears to be an even distribution of work among the three team members. If we assume that both this board and the previous one represent the progress of work over a similar period, we can also see that the team has accomplished more work on this second board than on the first one.

When the team has their next retrospective, they decide to continue the experiment for another month, to make sure it was not a fluke. What they observed was not only a decrease in quality issues but also an overall increase in productivity. They also expressed that they felt more like a team and have an increased sense of accomplishment.

## Limiting Work in Progress

There is a widespread belief that people are good at multitasking, even taking it so far as to be a badge of honor. This belief is so widespread that people frequently use *multitasking* as a buzzword on résumés. However, several studies have shown that people are very poor at multitasking. Anytime someone switches to a new activity, there is a loss of efficiency and effectiveness. Per the American Psychological Association's research, "Multitasking may seem efficient on the surface but may actually take more time in the end and involve more error. Meyer has said that even brief mental blocks created by shifting between tasks can cost as much as 40 percent of someone's productive time."[ii] It is the rare individual who is exceptional at minimizing lost time due to context switching. It is these exceptional individuals who give credence to the idea that multitasking is an effective practice. However, not everyone can be one of these select few, nor should we assume that every team we have will be made of individuals like this.

For most people, the most efficient and effective approach is to concentrate on one thing at a time. This has been proven time and again with different activities and experiments, yet this concept is difficult for some people to believe. I have spoken with people from extremely hectic call centers who believed that if they were not rotating between twenty things at once, they were not productive. People in situations like this become used to the hectic nature of the position. However, once they try working on only one thing at a time, they soon admit they are more productive than they thought was possible. This is a great example of challenging our assumptions and experimenting with an idea to see if it leads to improvements.

Still unsure about the whole multitasking thing? Do me a favor and try this. All you need is a stopwatch, three pieces of paper, and a pen or pencil. Begin by laying the three papers out in front of you, leaving the space directly in front of you empty. We will do two rounds for this experiment. In each round, we will end up with a square, triangle, circle, and diamond drawn on each piece of paper. For the first round, start the timer and immediately pull the first piece of paper in front of you and draw a square on it. Once you finish, put the paper back, pull the second one, and draw another square. Put this paper back, pull the third one, and draw a square on it as well. Once each paper has the square on it, go back to the first paper and repeat the above process, but this time draw a triangle. Repeat until all three pieces of paper have all four shapes. Once the drawings are complete, stop the timer and record how long it took you to complete the task. Now turn the papers over and reset the timer for a second round. Start the timer again, and this time, when you pull the first piece of paper in front of you, draw all four shapes. Then put it back, pull the second one, and repeat until the third piece of paper has all four shapes. Stop the timer, and record the time. How did the second time compare to the first? When teaching introductory classes on Agile, I find that my students will almost always record times almost twice as fast in the second round. This is just a simple example that reinforces how working on *one* thing at a time will make you more productive and effective. Imagine the time you would save if the tasks were more complex and took much longer to complete. This hidden cost of context switching is paid all day, every day, and eats away at our productivity and efficiency. By removing or alleviating this hidden cost, we can accomplish more work in less time on a regular basis.

There is an old saying in software development—*there is no such thing as a five-minute question*. Due to the nature of software development, this is more than just a saying. Software development requires focus, discipline, and the ability to solve complex problems programmatically. When someone interrupts this process to ask a question, context switching occurs. You will stop what you are doing and answer the question and afterward, it will take several minutes before you can resume your original thought process. Of course, this is not the only profession where this is true. Any profession that requires concentration will face the same challenges. The need to focus in an uninterrupted manner will manifest itself in multiple ways, like when team members close their office doors, by writers who seclude themselves into "busy" meetings to complete uninterrupted work, and by individuals who put on headphones the moment the workspace becomes noisy. Concentration is becoming increasingly important since distractions and complexity of problems are more apparent in today's workforce.

Different Agile frameworks try to limit the amount of work in progress in different ways. For example, one Agile framework, Scrum, limits how much work is brought into an iteration, while another framework called Kanban accomplishes this by allowing only so many work items in one state at a time. These concepts will be explained more when we review different Agile frameworks. For now, the point to drive home is that whichever framework you use, limiting the amount of work in progress is paramount for greater focus and increased throughput.

At their next retrospective, Sue's team talks about their current experiment to reduce quality issues, that it helps even more, when each of them is only working on one item at a time. This increased focus has allowed them to reduce quality issues even more.

## Working in Small Batches

As humans, we like to see progress. Think about this: Have you ever been downloading a file or installing an application and seen a progress bar that did not seem to be moving? How long did you wait before you thought to cancel the process and start again? Five minutes? Ten minutes? Conversely, even when we have an exceptionally long download or installation, we are normally quite happy to wait until it is completed as long as we see steady progress. This same desire for visible progress exists in our work life as well. So, if there is such a desire to see progress, why do we tend to work on items that require long periods of time to resolve? Typically, for the same reason we do not visualize the work. The normal tendency is to start the work right away and not take the time to break it down into smaller pieces. So, let's talk about the potential benefits of decomposing a work item into smaller pieces.

Breaking work items down to smaller pieces has several benefits. First, a team discussion around the work item increases the shared understanding of what needs to be accomplished in order to complete the item. This is extremely helpful for cross-training team members and preventing those silo-situations we all encounter, where work comes to a complete halt because one team member is unavailable to do the part that only he or she can do. It's also easier to estimate the duration of the smaller parts than the original large work item. If I were to ask you, how long do you think it would take you to walk across the room you are in, you likely would be fairly close to the real time it would take. If I then asked you, how long it would take to walk around the building you are in, I would guess that you would likely be off more than walking across the room. For a final round, if I asked you how long to walk two blocks and return, especially if you need to cross streets, I would be willing to bet your estimate would be off by a substantial amount. Try it for yourself, record your estimates and then time your walks. I was right, wasn't I? From the times I have run this experiment in my classes, it was very hard for the class to agree on a number for this last walk. This activity shows just how much easier and more accurate the estimate is when the task is smaller. A more accurate estimate also increases the chances of meeting expectations and delivering on time. As the team gets better at decomposing work and estimating, it's easier to forecast how long it might take the team to complete future deliveries. And this ties into the section we've already covered on *Visualize the Work*. Decomposition is beneficial since it increases the likelihood that more team members can work on the deliverable simultaneously, thus decreasing the total resolution time. These benefits encourage the team to work together and optimize the workflow.

One intangible benefit is the psychological effects that increased work flow can have on the team. Have any of you ever stared at the same item on your to-do list for months? Something that you know you need to accomplish but it's always just out of reach? It can be daunting and demoralizing. Similarly, when a work item is in progress for a long time, it can weigh on the team. Like the stalled download we discussed earlier, we begin to see it as something that will take forever, and we disengage from the task. We might continue to work on it, because we are supposed to, but we are no longer fully engaged, so it takes longer than it should. When the work is decomposed and the tasks can be completed quickly, even if the tasks are small, we get a sense of accomplishment. This, in turn, keeps us engaged, and the work gets done faster. "When you accomplish the goal you will get the dopamine-based sense of contentment and satisfaction that always accompanies the act of persevering and getting the job done," according to *Psychology Today*.[iii] This adds to a greater sense of job satisfaction, increased morale, and increased engagement for everyone on the team.

When we combine this tenet with visualizing the work, we can quickly see the improvements we get from breaking the work down into smaller pieces. The return on investment from the little bit of extra time up front to break down the work is returned in greater efficiency and predictability, more cross-training for the team, and overall higher morale as the team feels they are knocking the work out quicker and staying engaged longer.

Let's stop back in to see how Sue and her team are doing. Sue has been very pleased with the results from the team so far. Not only is the team producing more work, but they also seem happier and more connected with each other. At the last retrospective, the team implemented an experiment of breaking the items down to be smaller. The team completely surprised itself by how much stuff flew across the board that month. I think I heard them planning a surprise party for Sue for bringing this Agile approach into their work environment. Best of luck, team—great job!

# Part II: Secrets behind the Curtain

*True realism consists in revealing the surprising things which habit keeps covered and prevents us from seeing.*

—JEAN COCTEAU

*The true artist helps the world by revealing mystic truths.*

—BRUCE NAUMAN

# Being Agile

Now that we have gone over the basics, let's explore some of the more advanced benefits that Agile processes can provide an organization. It is not completely necessary that these topics sink in for now—they are a little harder to intuit, but I want to lay the groundwork, so that as you start to work with the basics, they will begin to make more sense.

It is possible to go through the motions of Agile without embracing the values underlying these practices. This is one of the hardest lessons we have learned in software development. When a group is just going through the motions, by performing the steps of a framework, without the values, they are just *doing* Agile. Once a team accepts the values and embraces them, I refer to them as *being* Agile. We will discuss more about different frameworks and options later. For now, it is important to understand that a framework will include processes and practices to help you start *doing* Agile. Once a team fully embraces the core values of the *Agile Manifesto* and starts *being* Agile, they will begin to reap the true benefits as well as have a strong enough basis to start customizing the framework to better enable them to succeed.

This small difference is the cause of most of the difficulties with switching to Agile. An Agile transformation is not just about changing the processes that are used; it is mostly a cultural change. To most people, change can be extremely unnerving, and cultural change even more than process changes. Most failures can be linked to a company trying to roll out Agile in a big-bang approach. This happens when the company or department announces, "As of today, we are Agile, and we will be using the X methodology." This can lead to failure because rushing a tremendous amount of cultural change at one time can cause a great deal of fear and angst. This can lead to people resisting the transformation, actively working against it, or even looking elsewhere for work. If this change can be rolled out slower, it will be more likely to succeed as teams will have the time to incorporate the Agile values.

Many organizations seek help from outside consultants to help with an Agile transition. The consultant will do his or her best to help educate teams and leadership on implementing the chosen Agile methodology. The person will teach Agile process and practices, while attempting to reinforce concepts with Agile values. This may seem to be a good approach, until the consultant must leave. From the consultant's view, he or she hopes the company has absorbed his or her teachings and is well on their way to continuing their journey to Agile. However, *lasting* cultural change is extremely difficult for one person to implement. Often, once the consultant moves on, old habits reemerge, leaving the company "going through the motions" without digging deeper and truly reaping the benefits of Agile.

For a successful Agile transformation, you need two things: executive buy-in and an Agile coach. There needs to be a leader with clout who supports and defends the processes. From personal experience, I can tell you that it is incredibly difficult to defend a transformation when deadlines are fast approaching and the pressure is on. It's very easy for management to suggest, "let's just go back to the way we're used to, get the work done, and once the dust settles, go back to using Agile." Huge mistake. Without this leadership support to hold true to the process, it will be put aside.

This sends a very strong signal to the team that Agile is not really accepted as the best approach, and makes returning to it after the dust settles that much harder.

The second is a knowledgeable Agile coach who is full time at the organization. This coach will have the time to continually work with teams and management on how to use the process to full effect and efficiency. It is of utmost importance that this coach understands the concept of "pulling and not pushing." While the coach needs to be available and always willing to help, he or she will not be as effective if he or she is seen as preaching or forcing Agile concepts on someone who may not be ready. This is crucial of a trained Agile coach: the ability to coach each person at the correct level to help him or her advance to the next level of understanding. Don't mistake that I am saying outside consultants or coaches are a bad idea. Reoccurring consultant visits can be very helpful to supplement and support the internal coaching. There is an old joke about how management "sometimes won't consider ideas unless they were brought to the table by someone from more than fifty miles away." Outside validation is sometimes needed to help jump the Agile culture of the company to the next level.

Without a strong commitment to the transformation, executive buy-in, and a dedicated Agile coach, a well-intentioned Agile transformation will most likely slowly degrade over time as teams abandon practices. Have you ever heard the phrase, "old habits die hard?" The same is true when making the cultural shift to Agile processes. Without dedication to the four tenets, it's easy for teams to cave to the "just get it done" mentality. Once these practices are abandoned, they are very hard to pick back up. The common result is an Agile implementation that is almost unrecognizable. Teams come to think that Agile doesn't work and are resistant to having someone tell them how to fix their processes later.

In a nutshell, Agile is easy to start but hard to maintain. It is like the game of chess, which has been said to take an hour to learn but a lifetime to master. The truth is that when Agile is done well, it is worth the effort to maintain it. It gives the organization a great advantage at staying in sync and keeping up with the changes in the market with less loss of momentum than their competition.

Finally, as you begin your Agile journey, it is important to suspend your disbelief. At first, much of what makes Agile work will appear counterintuitive. Remember that these are time-tested concepts that have been in practice for decades. Often, the ideas we think will work the least turn out to be the improvements we need the most. Don't be afraid to experiment or rule out ideas until you try them! As long as everyone is aligned in their desire to be better, for each other and the company, you will be able to continue to learn and improve. Setbacks are just that, a step back; however, each step back makes the next step forward easier.

## Journey More than a Destination

One of the leading causes of frustration from some Agile transformations is from the incorrect expectation that the transformation is a destination. When a reporter asked Thomas Edison, "How did it feel to fail one thousand times?" Edison replied, "I didn't fail one thousand times. The Light bulb was an invention with one thousand steps."[iv] As long as we learn from our failures, we can still use them to make improvements. Many companies go into one of these transitions expecting a consultant can make them Agile and then everything will work from that point on. This expectation exists partially because consultants will sell the idea of a transition, but mostly it is because the business does not fully understand that the Agile transformation is not the changes to the processes but rather the transformation of the culture and values the processes are built on.

Only when the business understands that the transformation is cultural and not procedural will it embrace the idea of the transformation being a journey. No matter which framework is chosen or how fast or slow the transformation is approached, any and all progress is beneficial. As the inspect-and-adapt cycle begins, teams will be making improvements and creating efficiency and effectiveness. So, it is the embracing of these values that gives organizations the true benefits of Agile.

Some of these cultural changes that need to be embraced are the encouragement of continuous learning, the willingness to fail fast, and continual experimentation. There are always improvements that can be made on any process. Often, the only thing holding us back from making improvements is that we do not know what our options are. No matter how much we know, there is always something more to learn. In addition, the more we learn, the more open to new learning and ways of thinking we become. Once we have everyone learning and thinking of new ideas, we need to be willing to fail. If we only try changes to our processes that we know for certain will make improvements, we will never change anything. The only way to know if a particular change will make an improvement is to try it and see. If the change is positive, we will adopt it. If it is not, we will discard it and try something else. However, we cannot do this if we are afraid that a failed experiment will be held against us in any way. This is why we need to be accepting of failure. Each failed experiment should be viewed as a learning opportunity. This is, of course, not a new idea. Now that we are encouraging experiments, we need to recognize that we should always be trying something new. This continual experimentation will allow us to always be making improvements and getting more efficient in everything we do.

## Continuous Learning

Humans are learning machines. As we continue to learn, we use our new-found knowledge as power to improve. This is true for both the individual and for groups. Rear Admiral Grace Murray Hopper once said, "The most damaging phrase in the language is 'We've always done it this way!'"[v] If we are not encouraged to learn and try new things, we will stagnate. When a company embraces learning, it opens doors for a culture of openness, innovation, and experimentation leading to greatly improved processes and practices.

On the same line, when we continually do the same type of work, we put ourselves in the mundane or the daily grind and stop challenging the status quo or thinking creatively. This is where a company that encourages learning can really benefit. Learning more about something close to what we work on can be extremely helpful. Even if the things we learn are not work related, the act of learning itself can assist us in breaking out of ruts and help drive innovative thinking. The old quote attributed to many people, including Anthony Robbins, Henry Ford, Mark Twain, and Albert Einstein, is especially apt: "If you always do, what you always did, you will always get what you always got." When we allow ourselves to stay nose to the grindstone, we do not have the time to think creatively and learn possible new ways to do things.

One of the best things a company can do to help itself improve is allow a little slack in the schedule so everyone has time to learn something new. Whether employees learn by watching how another department works, reading books, or taking classes, as the knowledge pool for the company increases, so does the likelihood that a new innovative approach can be discovered. This is true throughout the company and is not limited to any one field.

I know this may seem counterintuitive—that by allowing employees slack time, they will find ways to make themselves more productive. A good analogy to see this point a little better uses the image of an interstate. If the road is at 100 percent capacity without any slack, then it is loaded with stopped traffic, and no one can move. However, if the road is only at about 80 percent capacity, everyone can move along at the speed limit, or a little more, to be honest. This small amount of slack is important for many reasons, and using some of it to continue to learn is a great way of showing your employees that you value them and their personal development.

## Self-Organization

Decades of Agile implementation have shown us that by allowing the people in the trenches—the ones closest to the work—to figure out the best way to organize themselves and their work, they get more done. When the team comes together and cross-trains to become a high-performing unit, allowing them to self-organize will not only have the benefit of more informed and detailed decisions but also allow everyone to feel that he or she is part of the solution. This increases morale as well as engagement with the process. As each person engages in the process more, the chances for innovation and creativity increase.

Jeff Sutherland, a founding member of Scrum (an Agile framework) and signer of the Agile Manifesto, describes self-organization as one of the best secrets in that specific framework. I would expand on this and say that it applies to any form of Agile. A command-and-control management style assumes that a single person knows the strengths and weaknesses of team members and can correctly determine the best allocation of work to allow the team to be productive. This approach may make intuitive sense, but remember what I said earlier—Agile is not always intuitive. Like we've covered, the team knows best.

This approach allows managers more time to set strategic direction and develop team members. Agile managers have more time to keep big-picture initiatives in sight, removing impediments, helping with training needs, and encouraging best practices.

## Empowered Teams

With management support, teams can become empowered. This means that team members are given the authority and accountability to make their own decisions on how to get the work done. This allows decisions to be made quicker, unblocking the work faster than when the team needs to get decisions made by a higher authority. There are many advantages to this. Accountability will increase the amount of engagement among the team members. I remember an old interview with Richard Dean Anderson on the set of *Stargate SG-1*. He said that the best way to make sure that an actor shows up on time and knows his lines, is to make him an executive director.[vi] This, like so much else about Agile, is easy to say but harder to fully implement. However, once done this ability to increase the frequency and diversity of experimentation will help teams find innovative improvements. This is where the power of empowered teams truly shines.

A difficulty in reaching this level with a team is that empowerment is not something that can be given; it can only be supported. Telling a team that they are empowered doesn't make them so. The team themselves must take ownership of their work and improvements. It is only through the team claiming their empowerment that they uncover the benefits. It is vital for the management to fully support the team's effort to take this accountability as any pushback will slow down or halt the team's progress.

I would be amiss, if I did not let you know about a potential pitfall of empowered teams. When everyone can make decisions, it can sometimes be difficult to keep everyone going in the same direction without confusion. In order to mitigate this risk, it is important to have a clear chain of command. The escalation route to be taken when the team cannot agree on an approach is vital. It is also extremely important that the team is presented with a clear vision to help keep the big picture in mind.

## The Importance of Relative Sizing

Estimation is important for many reasons, but the main one is that it allows a way for a team to predict how fast they can deliver. Another reason that estimation is crucial, is without knowing which tasks are bigger than others, the team will not be able to work in small batches. We need to be able to identify the tasks that need to be broken down in order to improve our overall flow of work, as described earlier.

A normal tendency will be for the team to estimate how long an item will take. I can hear you now, what is wrong with that? We are wired to attempt to estimate in time, it's what we know and are used to. Have you ever needed to schedule a repair or installation at your home, and been given an estimate on when the technician will be at your house? Do you believe the estimate, or do you just take the day off to make sure you are there when the person finally arrives? In the software industry, we have a joke that if you ask a developer how long something will take, you'll most likely hear "Two weeks." Solving world hunger? "Two weeks." Putting an end to war? "Two weeks." Generally, we are unable to reliably predict how long something will take. This is compounded by the realization that the length of time a task will take will depend on which member of the team works on it. What might take one member of the team an hour could take another member hours or even days. So, when the team estimates how long something will take, who are they estimating for?

Remember the walk for a couple of blocks? You might not have been able to correctly guess the time, but I bet you knew it was more effort than to walk across the room, right? This is bigger than that, this is smaller, and these are about the same size. We excel at these types of comparisons. In order to get started with this, the team will need to pick a task that they feel is a normal size for the work they do. This becomes a reference point and base of comparison for tasks going forward. It is not important what units we use to measure our estimations as long as they are consistent. These abstract units should represent the complexity, effort, and risk of completing the item being estimated.

It is not common for a team to have everything they do to be of similar size. When this is the case, then teams can measure their progress by using the number of items that are processed and not worrying about estimating the items. Most of the time, however, work items will be different enough that we will need a way of estimating the sizes of individual items to get useful metrics.

Another typical practice is to use a nonlinear scale to determine the sizing. We use this since the larger the amount of work to be done, the less certainty there will be. An expanding scale accounts for this while decreasing the amount of discussion needed to get a team to a consensus on the size of a work item. There are a number of common methods to figure out the numbers for these estimation scales. The first method is to choose numbers from the binary scale. This means that each number is twice as big as the previous one. Acceptable values would be, one, two, four, eight, sixteen, thirty-two, and so on. A second and more common approach is to use the numbers from a Fibonacci sequence. This sequence is created by adding the previous two numbers in the sequence together. The sequence is, one, two, three, five, eight, thirteen, twenty-one, thirty-four, and so on. A slight modification has also been made to the Fibonacci sequence to help make remembering the numbers a little easier. This modified Fibonacci sequence is, half, one, two, three, five, eight, thirteen, twenty, forty, one hundred, and so on. This is such a common scale that you can buy decks of cards with this sequence for your team to use during the estimation process.

# Choosing a Framework

There are many different Agile frameworks an organization can choose to implement. Some are Scrum, Kanban, LeSS, XP, SAFe, and LEAN—just to name a few. According to the eleventh annual *State of Agile Report*[vii] released by VersionOne (an Agile-management tool provider), Scrum or one of its hybrids is used in 76 percent of companies that use Agile. The next most common implementation is Kanban and its hybrids, which are 13 percent. Please note that 8 percent of each is a Scrum/Kanban hybrid referred to as *Scrumban*. This means that these two frameworks, which we will discuss in more detail later, are used by 81 percent of companies that use Agile.

Each of these frameworks has advantages and disadvantages, and no one framework works best for everyone. This is where getting a good Agile consultant can help. The consultant should not have a bias of one framework over another. The person should be able to come in and evaluate the organization, the team, and the work to be done, and recommend the framework that will best match the environment.

Once a decision has been made on which framework to implement, you will need to set up the foundation and starting point for your Agile journey. The consultant can help here as well. You will need to decide if you are going to attempt a large scale, "Big Bang" approach where you convert the entire department at one time, or a slower soft launch by converting a single team. You will also need to arrange for training of everyone who will be changing processes to the new framework. You will also need to identify or begin training the internal Agile coach to assist in the transformation once the consultant needs to move on. Everyone will need to be trained on expectations. It is easy to see why the team needs to be trained, but anyone who interacts with the team also needs to be trained on how to work with them. This large-scale training is perfect for outside consultants, who can sometimes appear to have more credibility at this level of coaching than internal coaches. These outside consultants can also provide outside validation for the work the internal coaches provide.

There are several things Agile frameworks have in common. Among them are the four tenets we have already discussed. There are also slight differences that allow them to be customized for different teams. So, let's dig a little deeper into the most common frameworks and see how they provide a good base for companies that want to be Agile.

## Scrum

Scrum is the most common Agile framework implemented in business today. This framework is centered on formalized processes. This structured approach helps shelter teams while they try to learn Agile. There are prescribed roles and rituals that are defined to give the team a crutch to lean against, allowing them to begin to see some of the benefits of the new method even before the values driving it have been fully adopted.

There are three roles defined within Scrum: the team member, ScrumMaster, and product owner. The role of the team member is defined as anyone needed to produce deliverable work.

On a software-development team, this could include developers, quality-assurance testers, business analysts, database engineers, user-interface specialists, and writers. Team members in other departments would similarly be made up of everyone needed to reach his or her deliverable. For example, a financial team would be made up of accountants, auditors, and business analysts. Scrum teams are cross-functional, which helps them adjust to business needs better.

The ScrumMaster is responsible for ensuring that the team is upholding Agile best practices and working as efficiently as possible. In addition to coaching team members, ScrumMasters also coach managers and product owners toward Agile continuous improvement. If there is an impediment the team or a member on the team is facing, it is the responsibility of the ScrumMaster to alleviate the issue or escalate through the appropriate channels. The person facilitates team meetings, helping the team stay as effective and focused as possible. As the driver of continuous improvement on the team, the person often introduces new experiments aimed at increasing productivity, collaboration, and open communication.

The primary responsibility of the product owner is to ensure that high-value work is delivered to the customer as quickly as possible. He or she is the primary voice of the customers and stakeholders to the team. Product owners gather requirements and feedback from customers and relay that information to the team. They maintain a prioritized list of potential work items called a product backlog that is needed to complete a project. The product owners work with the team to estimate and break down work items. They also develop and manage release plans and track dependencies. It is often said that the product owner is the *single wringable neck*—who owns the release timeline and the backlog priorities. They are also the people who work the most with stakeholders and are responsible for making sure the highest value features are delivered as quickly as possible.

The Scrum process is designed to embrace the four tenets we've already discussed: making the work visible, inspect and adapt, limit work in progress, and work in small batches. In Scrum, teams work in a *sprint*, a predetermined amount of calendar time, between one to four weeks. Called *working in iterations*, it is important for each sprint to be of the same length to help the team learn from each cycle and improve each time. If the length of a sprint is ever changed, the team will need to create new baselines for improvement. At the beginning of the sprint, the team negotiates with the product owner to determine how much work they feel they can deliver by the end of the sprint. The items selected, preferably from the top of the product backlog, become the sprint backlog and are displayed on a sprint task-board. This task-board is how the work is visualized. During this process, work items are broken down by tasks so the team has a good understanding of everything that needs to be completed. Scrum uses the timebox of the sprint to limit the amount of work in progress. Forcing the work to be small enough to fit within a sprint abides the tenet for working in small batches.

In additional to planning the sprint, there are several other meetings called *ceremonies* the team attends. These meetings are typically facilitated by the ScrumMaster. Each day, the team meets for a *daily stand up* to plan how to get the most work done on the sprint backlog before the next daily meeting. They discuss what was completed yesterday, what they're planning on doing today, and any impediments that are blocking their progress. The standup is timeboxed to fifteen minutes. During the sprint, the team also meets with the product owner for a *backlog-refinement* meeting to help refine and estimate the items at the new top of the product backlog so it is prepared for the next sprint-planning meeting. At the end of the sprint, the team has a *sprint review*, where they demonstrate work they have completed to stakeholders with the goal of receiving feedback that can be incorporated into the product backlog. Sometimes this feedback will change the priority of the backlog. The last event of the sprint is the *sprint retrospective*. At this meeting, the team comes together to inspect the past sprint and determine what worked well and what can be improved. This meeting is the driving force for experimentation and continuous improvement.

Scrum uses just a handful of *artifacts* or tools to help with transparency of the progress of the project/product and sprint. The first is the *product backlog*. As discussed, this is a prioritized list of all the work that could be done for the product. The product owner owns not only the items in the backlog but also the responsibility to keep the backlog in priority order. The team will pull the top of this backlog into a smaller backlog called *sprint backlog*. This will be the work the team is committed to finishing in their current sprint. During the sprint, there is a report called a *sprint burndown*. This report helps identify how the team is doing in completing the sprint work on time. At the end of each sprint, quality work is delivered to the business and can potentially be delivered to customers. At this point, the product owner can also update a *project burndown* to allow for transparency on a project that will take multiple sprints to complete. This facilitates fast communication of project status. This early communication can also allow for the most time to come up with mitigation strategies if needed or discussions on changing the scope for release in order to make the dates.

Recently, *The Scrum Guide*[viii] was updated to include the Scrum values. These values are *openness, respect, focus, courage,* and *commitment.* These values are not only important for Scrum but are key for any Agile implementation. The five values are the building blocks that promote the success of the four tenets.

With Scrum's focused structure on meetings and artifacts, this is a fairly easy framework to implement. It requires fundamental understanding of the values of Agile, at least by the ScrumMaster and executive sponsors, to help keep the process on track when bumps in the road come along. The repeatable timebox of the sprint allows for very good predictability of when the team can deliver larger projects as well as regular check-ins of the project release plan.

# Kanban

Kanban is a very common but deceptive Agile framework. When first seen, Kanban can give the impression of not needing an actual process; and that the teams can just do what they want without planning or estimations. A correct implementation of Kanban relies on all team members having a very good understanding of the underlying Agile values. Unlike with Scrum, Kanban does not use a timeboxed iteration and has no predefined check-in points—planning and updates happen all the time. The main tool of Kanban is the *kanban board*. This is where all work is visualized and is the main method of communication both within and outside the team.

The simplest board setup, which was used by Sue and her team, contains *Not Started*, *In Progress*, and *Done* columns. The team can modify this layout to include any number of additional columns that will help make the workflow easier to use and see. If the team has someone who ultimately accepts that the work is done, then you might also add an *Accepted* column after *Done*. This could be a supervisor or someone filling in a role similar to that of the product owner in Scrum.

In Kanban, the roles described in the Scrum description can still be used and are often very beneficial. There still needs to be someone who owns the priorities of the work, and a product owner is a good choice for this role; the responsibilities between the two methods are almost the same. A ScrumMaster would also help, though he or she would likely be referred to by another name, for example, a team coach. No matter which name is used, the responsibilities are the same. The team coach needs to monitor and protect the process as well as coach the team toward improvements.

The board is how the Kanban framework demonstrates the tenet for visualization. By using the board and moving the cards across, the team can see how their process is working. Each of the columns on the board can have what is referred to as a WIP limit. This stands for *work in progress* and is a limit to how many items can be in that state or column at one time. Using the WIP limits forces team members to stay focused and not work on too many things at one time.

Kanban also focuses on cycle time. *Cycle time* is a measure of how long a work item stays within a state. To help improve cycle time, teams are encouraged to decompose work items as much as it makes sense to. This decreases cycle time and increases the flow of work across the board.

The main driver of continuous improvement in Kanban is elimination of waste in the process. For this method to be effective, the team needs to be very self-motivated, and responsible for keeping the board up to date. They also need to be very focused. Once a team member starts a work item, he or she should finish it before starting another item, even if higher priority items are added to the board. Although Kanban does not have a prescribed time for retrospectives, I recommend a regularly scheduled time to inspect and adapt the processes you are using. This will give the team the opportunity to experiment with ways of eliminating waste, decreasing cycle time, and increasing the flow of items across the board.

The extreme benefits you can get from the Kanban framework require a good understanding of Agile values. However, since the Kanban board itself is so intuitive to use, it can be used to help a department or team into Agile without a big transformation effort. Change can be scary to some people, and a lot of change at once can be even scarier. By using the Kanban board to just practice the tenets of Agile, we can perform a soft launch of Agile values without introducing a great deal of change at one time. We accomplish this by using the board to visualize the work being done without changing any other processes. I still highly recommend having a knowledgeable Agile coach on hand to assist with encouraging the Agile values and the remaining tenets as the team becomes ready for them. As the team becomes accustomed to each new change, the coach can introduce the next improvement idea. We will discuss this progression in more detail later.

# Part III: Where Do We Go from Here?

*Success is a process…During that journey sometimes there are stones thrown at you, and you convert them into milestones.*

—SACHIN TENDULKAR

*So it's been kind of a long road, but it was a good journey altogether.*

—SIDNEY POITIER

# Look Out! Hazards Ahead

We have talked about how Agile is the scientific method applied to business practices. We also discussed the underlying values that are needed for a group to be Agile. We then moved on to some more advanced topics on what it means to be Agile and some of the more common frameworks that can be applied.

I have stated multiple times that the concepts we are discussing are not complicated. In fact, they are simple. They take extraordinary discipline to keep with them in light of everyday pressures and time lines. If we can hold fast to our goals and the long-term vision, we can gain great benefits.

However, I don't want to give the impression that everything is wine and roses. There are, in fact, several pitfalls and bumps in the road that you should look out for. In this section, we will discuss some of the more common difficulties of implementing an Agile culture or framework. We will conclude this part with a suggested progression that could be used to slowly introduce your team or department to Agile and begin your own journey as a team.

## Team Makeup

Small departments will likely just have everyone be part of the same team. Most departments, however, will have enough people to have more than one team. Teams should be between three and nine people, with a preferred size of five to seven. In special circumstances, teams of fewer than three can exist, as long as the team still has all the skills needed to do the work. Three people are normally considered the minimum required to ensure the team has all the skills needed for a quality delivery of complex work. Nine people should be considered a very large team, as it is hard for so many people to stay synchronized with one another. A team of nine would likely function better as a team of five and another of four.

The Agile team should consist of everyone needed to complete the work for the deliverable, the product owner, and the coach. This ensures that not only does the team have the members to do the work, but they also have the support structure to ensure they can work effectively and continually make improvements.

Once the teams are established, they should remain intact for as long as possible to improve their efficiency. It takes a while for a new team to fully come together, and the gains from a team working well together should not be underestimated. If the business needs to change directions, instead of breaking the team up, the team should be moved as a unit to the new project, maintaining the working arrangement the business has invested in.

As much as you want to keep the teams together to maximize the investment in them, eventually they need to be changed up a little to keep them from getting complacent. This normally takes about fourteen to eighteen months. At this time, a small change should be made to shake things up just enough to break the team out of any rut, yet minimize the amount of time needed for the team to return to a performing state.

# The Advantage of T-Shaped Team Members

One of the most powerful concepts of Agile teams is that the team has all the skills needed to deliver finished, high-quality work. This often requires that team members have different skills that complement one another. A frequent approach, is to encourage that the work goes from one team member to the next so everyone maintains his or her areas of expertise. This type of team makeup is commonly referred to as having *I*-shaped members because each member has a depth of understanding on his or her specialty but little to no understanding of anyone else's skill set. The driving force behind this idea is that if everyone is an expert in his or her area, the team is completely balanced. But what if a team member takes a vacation or sudden leave of absence? Chances are, if everyone is specialized, no one will be able to cover for the team member who is out. Also, as backlog items are also unpredictable, sometimes there will be an abundance of one type of work, causing a team member to be overworked while the others may not have enough to keep busy.

The idea of keeping team members in personal silos of information also makes it difficult for the team to truly own a shared commitment of getting work done. The best way for a team to protect against the inevitable imbalances is to allow their members to cross-train one another so at least the basic understanding of each person's specialty is understood by someone else on the team. This would help the team still deliver the work promised even if a key person was out. The rest of the team might have a more difficult time, but they can come together, fill in the gap, and maintain the delivery. This cross-training also increases the team's sense of self and encourages them to work more like a true team and not just a group of people working on similar items.

This cross-training of team members produces teams made up of what is normally referred to as *T*-shaped members. Each member not only maintains understanding on his or her specialty but also begins to broaden his or her understanding to key skills of other team members. This approach to team makeup is more valuable to companies in the long run. As most work in complex systems are ever changing, having a team of people who can quickly adapt to business needs is a far better long-term investment.

## The Dangerous Seduction of Hybrids

A very common practice when companies transition is to have people perform more than one role in their Agile implementation to save head count and money. At first glance, this might appear to be a good move when the company is unsure if Agile will work for them. But let's look back at one of the tenets we mentioned earlier—limit work in progress. The core of limiting work in progress is to do one thing well instead of trying to do two things just OK. Someone in a *hybrid role* is being asked to do two roles at the same time.

One of the most common hybrids is the developer-coach combination. A reason this hybrid is so attractive at first glance for most companies is because the Agile transformation normally begins as a grassroots change. This means that a team takes it upon itself to become more Agile. A member of the team will take on the product owner's responsibilities (see below), and another will take on the responsibilities of the coach. This allows a team to start gaining the benefits of Agile even before they have manager buy-in to the process. Even if the change has buy-in from a middle manager, the team can still take this path as they do not have authorization yet to increase head count to prove that Agile will work.

There are several disadvantages to this combination, however. First is that most developers, whether programmers, accountants, or any other persons who delivers the work of the team, are in that position because it is what they want to do. Even if the developer chooses to step up to the hybrid role, the responsibilities of the coach will begin to chaff as it pulls him or her away from where his or her true passion is, developing. This is often compounded by managers who will continue to evaluate the person solely on his or her original job function. This encourages the person to spend as little time as possible acting as coach, reducing the benefits of having the role and decreasing the benefits of Agile in the process. Whether you are using Scrum or another framework, having someone monitor and facilitate the process as well as drive continuous improvements is extremely valuable. To diminish the use of this role makes success with the Agile process much more difficult.

The other possibility of this hybrid is that the person assigned to the role feels more connected to the coach part of it. There will still be some pull away from the coach role as some development still needs to be done, but enough will remain that the coach role is effectively covered. This means, of course, that the person is doing very little as a developer on the team, which decreases the throughput. This may be acceptable depending on the number of team members and the type of work being done. If so, it would still be better to allow the person to transition fully to the coach role and backfill the developer position he or she left.

Most non-Agile projects will already have someone determining the direction the team will take. The second hybrid we will talk about is not as common as the developer-coach but still happens for many of the same reasons. This is when one of the developers on the team begins to take on some of the prioritization of the work being done by the team. This hybrid of the product owner and developer suffers the same issues as the developer-coach hybrid. This combination normally has a bigger impact on the amount of work produced by the team as it is normally the most knowledgeable team member who fills in for the product-owner responsibilities. Even if the organization already has someone providing direction, it is normally at a very high level and not refined to allow the team to be the most productive. This valuable duty is performed by the product owner, and maintaining a healthy and refined backlog of work ready for the team to start is vital to the team's efficiency. However, to lose your most knowledgeable team member to keep the backlog in this desired state greatly reduces the team's throughput.

Another common hybrid is the coach-product owner. This combination does not distract from the team doing the work like the previous two hybrids but still leaves someone in a difficult position. In the product-owner role, the person is expected to maintain the backlog and try to get the team to deliver as much as possible as quickly as possible. This agenda is sometimes, if not often, at odds with coaching the team to work at a sustainable pace and to take time to improve their processes to allow for faster delivery in the long run. It is extremely difficult to be completely fair to both sides of this hybrid, and we often see, as before, that one side or the other suffers.

Some of the difficulties mentioned for the coach-product owner hybrid are similar to when the product-owner role is performed by the same person who is also the team members' manager. This combination is even harder because of the authority that comes with the manager position. It is difficult for a team to fully negotiate the amount or speed of the work with the product owner when that person is the same one who will evaluate them for promotion and bonuses. The most common result is that the team will not push back or negotiate commitments. This will stifle self-organization and engagement as well as the innovation and creativity that come with it. Likewise, when the coach role is being handled by the manager, his or her advice and suggestions are now perceived as commands. The monitoring and reporting that the coach role does, in order to keep the team informed of the effects of experimentation or areas for improvements, can be seen as attempts to "weaponize" the metrics. At which time the teams will likely start filling in the numbers they think the manager wants instead of what is really going on. This completely erodes the benefits of monitoring and reduces the benefits of Agile by obscuring what improvements could be helpful.

For smaller teams, the hybrid of a product owner and project manager can actually work very well. If the projects are small enough, having a single person with all this knowledge helps keep the backlog and priorities optimized. The problem comes in when the projects are not small enough or are in a very complex field. It can become a full-time responsibility, as a project manager, just to keep up with the market and direction the product should take, not allowing enough time to do the team-level work-item maintenance the team needs to maintain their productivity and effectiveness.

The worst hybrid pattern that can be used is when the same person is expected to act as product owner, manager, and coach. The conflicts of interests listed above are compounded on one another in this situation, making it almost impossible for the person to do any of the roles effectively. The most common result of this hybrid is that the team devolves into chaos with very little productivity and a great deal of frustration for everyone. This is normally because the priorities are not well maintained, and the team goes into firefighting mode and never seem to get their heads above water as the priorities constantly shift around them.

The main lesson to be learned from this section is that each of these roles plays a vital part in helping the team increase their productivity. If done right, they are more than full-time positions and worth the overhead cost involved with having the positions filled. If a company wants to maximize cost without too much loss of efficacies, the roles of manager, coach, and product owner can be spread across multiple teams. These roles can cover two teams without much reduction in efficiency, especially if the teams are working on the same or similar projects.

# Next Steps

Our journey will now come to a fork in the road. From here, there are many paths you can take. So, let's take a look at the first steps of some of these paths so we can help you choose. As a first step, you are going to need a good Agile coach. This could be someone internal to the company who wants to transition into the position or someone hired from outside. An outside consultant can be extremely helpful for large-scale education on the process you would like to use as well as for training your Agile coach. The coach will need to either have or quickly gain the required knowledge to help lead and support the transition as it goes along.

In addition to a coach, you will need to ensure you have executive support for the transition. If management is not behind the transition, it will be severely difficult to get most of the benefits of Agile. On the flip side, if there is good management support of the effort, the teams will have a much better chance of success, no matter which path you take.

The first and easiest path is to do nothing. It is possible you have gotten to this part in the book and decided this Agile stuff is not for you. That is OK. Although I believe everyone can benefit from Agile, it is not for everyone. I hope I have been able to give you some insights into those who use it and that it will help with your interactions with them.

A second and common path is to attempt a transition to Scrum. There are several very good books and classes on Scrum. There are also a great many consultants who can help with an Agile transition using this approach. The benefits of having a defined process can make the transition easier. Scrum is typically best when used for complex work. If you are doing this type of work with plenty of unknowns, then this might be a good choice. If the work you are doing is less complex, then another path might be better. I do want to make something clear—less complex does not mean less important. There are plenty of important things we do that we clearly understand how to do.

If the work you are doing is less complex, then perhaps Kanban is a better approach for you. It has the benefit of being more intuitive and less intrusive to the current way of working. There are also a good number of consultants out there to help with a transition. Kanban is a great way to visualize the work and attempt to eliminate waste.

There is also a path that combines both of these. It is normally referred to as Scrumban. This approach uses a Kanban-like board but uses an iteration timebox like Scrum. It has some of the more flexible behavior of Kanban but also regular check-in points. Like all paths, this one has its advantages and disadvantages. If this path appeals to you, then I would suggest more research into it.

The last approach we will discuss is what I referred to earlier as a soft launch. We have already discussed the difficulties in a big-bang approach toward an Agile transition. A softer approach, especially outside of software-development departments, can yield a much higher success rate.

Once the support structure is in place, you can begin your transition with the easiest tenets and work your way to include all of them. We'll start with just making the work visible. We discussed earlier the simplest form of a Kanban board. This has a *Ready*, *In Progress*, and *Done* column. The idea is to have the team start using the board and not change anything else about their processes. Create cards to represent each of the work items the team does, and add them to the board. Have the team members move the cards across the board to reflect the current progress as they work on them. Do not make any other changes to the process at this stage.

Once the team is used to the board, you can set up a regular scheduled time for the team to evaluate how things are going. Having this time to inspect and adapt will be extremely valuable. It establishes the continuous-improvement engine for the team. Fully primed by the team using the board, the coach should be able to immediately start helping the team find improvements. Among the first couple will likely be the remaining tenets of limiting work in progress and working in small batches.

From here, the team can continue on this way, making improvements to their process. They could also adopt a full Kanban process or even switch over to Scrum, depending on the work they are doing. The important thing is that with each inspect-and-adapt cycle, the team should gain a better understanding of the core values underlying these new processes. With the help of the coach, the team should make steady progress.

# Epilogue

I hope you have enjoyed our journey into the world of Agile. We began with some basic underlying values common to all Agile implementations. We then expanded to include some conversation about two of the most common methodologies used to implement Agile. We also covered some of the major issues and common mistakes in attempting a transition. We ended with discussions on possible next steps to help you decide what to do from here, including a method to soft launch an Agile progression that might be a good choice to increase your chances for success.

This book was intended to give you an introduction to a subject that has been covered in many books. If you would like more details on any particular methodology, please continue your reading for more information.

It is my sincerest wish that this book has helped you better understand what Agile is and how you can use it. Keep true, have courage, expand your knowledge, and experiment continually, and you will always find a better way to do whatever you need to do. This will not only lead to increased morale for your team and company but also give your company a great advantage in its market, as you will be able to more easily adjust to our changing times.

# About the Author

Al Kraus is an Agile Coach, lead ScrumMaster, and mentor with more than ten years of experience transforming Agile teams, whose credits include: Certified ScrumMaster (CSM), Certified Scrum Product Owner (CSPO), and Certified Scrum Professional (CSP) from Scrum Alliance. Additionally, he is a certified Scrum@Scale practitioner from Scrum Inc. and holds an ICAgile Certificated Professional—Agile Coaching designation.

He is a strong advocate for continual learning and experimentation. Through his tenure at multiple companies, he continues to push himself and his teams for ongoing growth and improvement. Kraus worked as a software developer and ScrumMaster for Rosetta Stone for more than nine years. During this time, he also taught night classes at National College in Harrisonburg, Virginia, which fortified his desire to teach others and see them advance. Since 2013, he has been with Video Gaming Technologies, Inc.—an Aristocrat Company.

Building on his credentials as an engaging instructor and facilitator, Kraus created multiple classes aimed at expanding Agile adoption outside the software development and information-technology departments. Encouraging creativity and a think-outside-the-box mentality, he developed the Agile Community of Practice at VGT, along with innovation and technological showcase events. Kraus has facilitated multiple Open Space events to improve alignment as well as executive strategic-planning meetings.

Kraus lives with his wife, Karen, and their daughter, Julie, in Nashville, Tennessee. They share their house with their two cats, Tessa and Charlie, and their new puppy, Bella. In addition to his unquenchable thirst for knowledge, he enjoys movies, digital painting, and developing his own computer games.

Linked in https://www.linkedin.com/in/alfredmkraus

# Endnotes

i.  "Manifesto for Agile Software Development," accessed May 22, 2017, http://agilemanifesto.org/.

ii.  "Multi-tasking: Switching costs," American Psychological Association, accessed May 25, 2017, http://www.apa.org/research/action/multitask.aspx.

iii.  "The Neuroscience of Perseverance," *Psychology Today*, accessed May 26, 2017, https://www.psychologytoday.com/blog/the-athletes-way/201112/the-neuroscience-perseverance.

iv.  "But They Did Not Give Up," accessed May 26, 2017, https://www.uky.edu/~eushe2/Pajares/OnFailingG.html.

v.  "Most Dangerous Phrase: We've Always Done It That Way," Quote Investigator, accessed May 25, 2017, http://quoteinvestigator.com/2014/11/27/always-done/#note-10178-4.

vi.  "Behind the Scenes, DVD Extras," *Stargate SG-1 Season 1* Complete set.

vii.  "11th Annual *State of Agile Report*," VersionOne, posted April 6, 2017, https://explore.versionone.com/state-of-agile/versionone-11th-annual-state-of-agile-report-2.

viii.  Ken Schwaber and Jeff Sutherland, "The Scrum Guide," accessed May 25, 2017, last updated July 2016, http://www.scrumguides.org/docs/scrumguide/v2016/2016-Scrum-Guide-US.pdf.

Made in the USA
Middletown, DE
29 October 2017